SCHOLASTIC

Revision
Grade 5
Mini-Lessons

By Sarah Glasscock

NEW YORK • TORONTO • LONDON • AUCKLAND • SYDNEY
MEXICO CITY • NEW DELHI • HONG KONG • BUENOS AIRES

Teaching *Resources*

Cover Design by Jaime Lucero

Interior Design by Sydney Wright

Interior Illustrations by Kelly Kennedy

ISBN-13: 978-0-439-70489-2
ISBN-10: 0-439-70489-8
Copyright © 2006 by Sarah Glasscock
Printed in the U.S.A.

1 2 3 4 5 6 7 8 9 10   40   14 13 12 11 10 09 08 07 06

CONTENTS

INTRODUCTION

One of the most difficult things about writing is making sure that we have successfully translated the ideas in our head to the words on the page. The goal in writing is to communicate effectively so that the reader is transported and not disappointed or confused. Revising is an essential part of the writing process. By going over what we've written, we show ownership of and pride in our words.

How to Use This Book

Each lesson contains a passage with errors for students to revise. A variety of genres, and curriculum links, are represented in the passages. To serve as a reference for students, a cartoon and a reminder about a key aspect of the topic appear above each passage. The first error in each passage is corrected on the page. When you begin teaching these lessons, I suggest that you read aloud the passage as students follow along. By using the rhythm of your voice and intonation, you'll be able to highlight the errors in a passage, for example, making your delivery flat as you read a series of repeated nouns or stumbling over misspelled words.

The corresponding teaching page contains a bulleted list of common errors associated with the topic, a review section called Replay, troubleshooting tips, and a section with

suggestions about how to present the passage and model the correction shown. These are only suggestions—feel free to tailor the lesson to the needs of your students and your own teaching style.

After you and your students have discussed the passage, it's their turn to become editors. There is space for them to mark their changes directly on the passage reproducible. A checklist appears at the bottom of this page as a guide for students. Before students copy their revision on the blank reproducible page, have them write it out on a separate sheet of paper. This will give them some leeway to revise a bit more before they actually publish their final draft.

Sample revisions appear in an answer key at the back of the book, along with a writing checklist. There is a list of proofreader's marks on page 5. Make sure students are familiar with and comfortable using the proofreader's marks before they tackle the passages.

Encourage your students to make these passages their own. Although the focus of a passage may be on subject-verb agreement, students should make any other changes they feel would strengthen the passage.

I hope this book helps your students— and you—feel that revision can be a pleasure.

Proofreader's Marks

Symbol	Meaning	Example
∧	Add a word or phrase	The ∧ puppy sighed. *(lonely)* The puppy sighed∧. *(in his sleep)*
൮	Delete a letter or a word	The dark chocolate brown puppy yappⴝed. The ~~deep, dark~~ chocolate brown puppy yapped.
≡	Capitalize	The active puppies at pet world tumbled in their pen.
/	Lowercase	My ⌀ad brought home a Border Collie puppy.
∽	Transpose letters	Border collies are one of the smartest breesd of dogs.
⊙ ⑦ ⑪	Change end punctuation	Do you have any pets∧ *(?)* I have two dogs and three hamsters∧ *(.)*
¶	Begin a new paragraph	¶My dog, Buster, loves to jump on the couch. He enjoys watching TV with me.

Working Together: SUBJECT-VERB AGREEMENT

Passage "Christmas Eve in Death Valley" (nonfiction)

Curriculum Area Social Studies

Subjects and verbs must work together in a sentence. When students revise their work, they have to make sure the subjects and verbs still agree with each other.

Your students may encounter the following problems with subjects and verbs in their writing:

- Omitting a subject or a verb in a sentence.
- Choosing the wrong form of a verb to go with a subject.
- Difficulty identifying compound subjects and compound verbs.

Replay

Briefly review the singular and plural forms of some regular and irregular nouns and verbs. Then, write some nouns (common and proper) and verbs on the board and ask students to create simple sentences with the words—for example, *Mice* <u>*scamper*</u>, <u>*Chocolate*</u> *has oozed.* Be creative in your word choices, and encourage your students to do the same. As students share their sentences, ask other members of the class to identify the subjects and verbs and to verify their agreement.

Troubleshoot

Share these tips with your class.

✓ Imperatives—*Go! Tell me.*—are complete sentences. The subject *you* is understood—*You go! You tell me.*

✓ In a sentence like *Each of the dogs comes when I call,* students often confuse *dogs* as the subject instead of *Each.* Remind them to pull out the phrase *(of the dogs),* and then identify the subject and verb in the remaining sentence *(Each comes when I call).*

✓ Students will encounter sentence fragments in published works of fiction and nonfiction. Writers often use fragments for emphasis or to indicate stream-of-consciousness. You may want to broach the subject yourself and bring in several examples. After students read the examples, talk about why they think each author chose to use fragments instead of complete sentences. Challenge them to revise the writing to include complete sentences and then to compare the revisions to the original work.

Which do they think conveys the author's message better? Some students will certainly ask why they can't use fragments in their own writing when published writers can. Explain that these authors worked hard to master the fundamentals of sentences before experimenting with their form.

Model

After distributing the passage "Christmas Eve in Death Valley," read it aloud as students follow along on the reproducible. Discuss the content with them. Then, point out that the passage contains many errors in subject and verb agreement. What were students' reactions to the errors? Did they notice the errors as you read the passage? Did the errors cause confusion? You may want to talk about how the errors affected your reading of the work.

Think aloud to show how and why the correction on the page was made. You might say something like the following: *The first error in subject and verb agreement appears in the third sentence. I see that the sentence has a compound subject—Deserts and mountains. Since both of the subjects are plural—and they are joined by the word "and"—I know that the verb should also be plural. However, the verb shown in the sentence is not plural; it's singular. The writer should have used "stand" instead of "stands."*

As students complete the revision on their own, circulate among them to answer any questions and to spot those who may be having problems completing the task.

Name _____   Date _____

Working Together: **Subject-Verb Agreement**

Read the following nonfiction passage.

Remember: A singular noun always takes a singular verb. A plural noun always takes a plural verb.

Christmas Eve in Death Valley

The year is 1849. Gold has been discovered in California. It isn't easy for the Forty-Niners, the people heading west to make their fortunes, to reach California. Deserts and the High Sierra Mountains stands between them and California—and nobody wants to get trapped in the Sierras by heavy snowfall.

The members of one wagon party to take a chance. Instead of waiting all winter in Salt Lake City and then crossing the mountains, they decide to take the Old Spanish Trail around the mountains. Unfortunately, no wagon train have ever tried this route— and only one person in Salt Lake City know the trail. Still, the 120 wagons head out, moving slowly—too slowly for some people. When a man rides into camp and show them a map with a shortcut, almost everyone decides to take another chance. The shortcut would take 500 miles off their trip. Who wouldn't agree to that?

Soon, the group face Beaver Dam Wash near the present-day border of Utah and Nevada. The sight of this canyon is enough to send 100 wagons back to the Old Spanish Trail. After the remaining 20 wagons make it through the canyon, trouble strike again. The man—and his map—disappear from camp! Still, the group decides to keep heading west across the desert.

On Christmas Eve, the Forty-Niners camp near springs that spout more than 2,000 gallons of water a minute. They've been traveling across the desert for more than two months. As they leave the springs, one man looks back and says, "Good-bye, Death Valley!" What he don't know is that the worst part of the trip still lies ahead. Standing in their path is a wall of mountains.

Do you see any problems in this passage? Does each sentence contain a subject and a verb? Do the subjects and the verbs agree with each other?

Is the writing as clear as it could be?

Reread the passage. Then, mark any changes you would make. The first change has been made for you.

Working Together: **Subject-Verb Agreement**

Read the checklist at the bottom of the page. Then, go over your revision of "Christmas Eve in Death Valley" once more. Copy it on the lines below.

_____

_____

_____

_____

_____

_____

_____

_____

_____

_____

_____

_____

_____

_____

_____

_____

_____

_____

_____

_____

_____

_____

_____

Checklist

❏ Is each sentence complete?

❏ Does it contain a subject and a verb?

❏ Does each verb agree with its subject?

❏ Have you correctly identified the subject of each sentence?

Revision Mini-Lessons • Grade 5 • Scholastic Teaching Resources

It or Them?: NOUN-PRONOUN AGREEMENT

Passage "Can I Have Another Slice?" (realistic fiction)

Curriculum Area Language Arts

What would we do without pronouns? We'd be forced to keep using the same nouns over and over again, which would affect the variety and flow of our speech and writing.

Your students may encounter the following problems when they replace nouns with pronouns in their writing:

- Choosing the wrong pronoun.
- Neglecting to balance the usage of nouns and pronouns.
- Failing to make sure the reader knows to whom or what the pronoun refers.

Replay

For a quick review, copy this chart of subject and object pronouns on the board. As you go through the chart, ask volunteers to supply sentences for the pronouns. You also may want to go over possessive pronouns with your students.

Subject Pronouns		Object Pronouns	
Singular	**Plural**	**Singular**	**Plural**
1st person: I	1st person: we	1st person: me	1st person: us
2nd person: you	2nd person: you	2nd person: you	2nd person: you
3rd person: he, she, it	3rd person: they	3rd person: him, her, it	3rd person: them

Singular Possessive Pronouns	Plural Possessive Pronouns
1st person: my	1st person: our
2nd person: your	2nd person: your
3rd person: his, her, its	3rd person: their

Then, write the sentences below on the board. Have students copy them on a sheet of paper. They'll be revising each sentence, so ask them to leave several blank lines between each one. *"Sean wants to attend camp so Sean can learn to play the drums," Sean explained to Sean's mother. Although Sean already played the trumpet in the band, Sean didn't seem to enjoy playing the trumpet. Sean's mother asked Sean what Sean wanted to do during Sean's summer vacation. The door to Sean's room was open, and Sean's mother could hear Sean tapping Sean's pencil on Sean's desk.*

Ask students to revise each sentence, changing some nouns to pronouns. Then, challenge students to cut apart the sentences and put them together to form a story. What do they think of their pronoun choices now? Do the choices still make sense, or would they like to revise the sentences again?

Troubleshoot

Share these tips with your class.

✓ Some contractions are formed using pronouns and verbs—*I'm, I've, he'll, she'd, it's, they're,* and so on. Emphasize the importance of the apostrophe: It takes the place of the letter or letters that are dropped. Remind students that *it's* is a short form of *it is* and that *its* is a possessive pronoun.

✓ Students often have trouble recognizing that nouns such as *class, group,* and *family* are singular and should be replaced with the pronoun *it* rather than *they.* Ask students to use these nouns in a sentence, and then have them identify the singular verbs they paired with the nouns.

Model

Read aloud the passage "Can I Have Another Slice?" to your students. After discussing its content, ask students how the passage sounded to them. Did the words seem to flow smoothly? Did any of the language seem repetitious or boring?

Then, ask students to read the passage silently. After they finish, walk them through the correction given on the page. You might say something like this: *The narrator is helping Mr. Baines push the dough into the pan; he or she [the narrator] doesn't mention anyone else besides Mr. Baines. It seems clear to me that the narrator means only Mr. Baines. The writer should have used a singular pronoun to replace the proper noun Mr. Baines. The writer should have used "him" instead of "them." Remember that a pronoun always takes the place of a specific noun. To make sure which pronoun to use, we always have to know exactly which noun is being replaced.*

After allowing time for students to read the passage independently, work with the whole class to revise the story. Continue modeling as necessary, and then let students take over the process

It or Them?: **Noun-Pronoun Agreement**

Read the following story.

Reminder: Be sure to replace a singular noun with a singular pronoun and a plural noun with a plural pronoun.

Can I Have Another Slice?

A white cloud puffed out of the cement mixer as Mr. Baines emptied the last 50-pound sack of flour into the cement mixer. Soon, pizza dough chugged out of the machine. "I told you math could be fun," Mr. Baines shouted to me as I helped ~~them~~ ^him^ push the dough to the edges of the specially made pan.

Bettina opened the last huge can of tomato sauce. "I can't believe how sore my arm is," Bettina said. "Who knew that slicing 20 pounds of mozzarella cheese and five pounds of pepperoni could be such hard work?" (Bettina's parents owned a grocery store, and it had donated the tomato sauce, so it was only right that Bettina should get to open the last can.)

The idea of making a super-size pizza came up in Mr. Baines's math class. (It must be the hungriest class in the entire school.) We students figured that we'd be able to cut our pizza into 225 slices. If we sold each slice for two dollars, I'd be able to raise almost $500 for the school library.

Jacob and Madison used brand-new mops to spread tomato sauce on his side of the dough. Then I threw pepperoni rounds on top of the pizza as if I were throwing me Frisbee. Bettina stood beside I and tossed handfuls of grated cheese on top of the pizza.

The pizza tasted great, and we sold every slice. In fact, I bought and ate six slices. Just don't expect me to be having pizza anytime soon.

Do you see any problems in the passage? Have the nouns been replaced with the correct pronouns? Does the passage contain a good mix of nouns and pronouns?

Is the writing as clear as it could be?

Reread the passage. Then, mark any changes you would make. The first change has been made for you.

Revision Mini-Lessons • Grade 5 • Scholastic Teaching Resources

It or Them?: **Noun-Pronoun Agreement**

Read the checklist at the bottom of the page. Then, go over your revision of "Can I Have Another Slice?" once more. Copy it on the lines below.

_____

_____

_____

_____

_____

_____

_____

_____

_____

_____

_____

_____

_____

_____

_____

_____

_____

Checklist

❏ Have you used the correct pronoun to replace each noun?

❏ Does the revised passage contain a variety of nouns and pronouns?

❏ Do the pronouns you substituted for nouns make your meaning clear?

Onward to the Past: VERB TENSES

Passage "Coyote: Fact and Myth" (nonfiction and fiction)   **Curriculum Area** Science and Social Studies

Changing the tense of a verb is like traveling in time. An incorrect shift in tense can send you flying into the future or the past—when all you wanted to do was stay in the present.

Your students may encounter the following problems with verb tenses in their writing:

- Using the incorrect verb tense with time markers.
- Changing verb tenses within a sentence or a paragraph.
- Omitting part of a verb in a sentence.

Replay

Review the simple verb tenses, using examples of regular and irregular verbs, such as *walk* and *go*. Also list some common auxiliary verbs on the board or an overhead transparency, including *am, is, are, was, were, been, do, does, did, has, have, had, shall*, and *will*. Ask students to create verb phrases composed of auxiliary verbs and forms of the main verbs *walk* or *go*. Point out that auxiliary verbs, like main verbs, must agree with the subject. Then, challenge students to use their verb phrases in sentences. You also may want to review common time markers such as *yesterday, today, tomorrow, at that time, now, for the next two years, before, already, by this time tomorrow.*

For more practice, challenge students with this writing activity. Form three groups and give each one a time-sensitive name such as *Yesterday, Today*, or *Tomorrow*. Have students collaborate on a short paragraph using the verb tense that corresponds to their group name. Everyone will write on the same topic. Suggest something as straightforward as writing about a school event or as exotic as imagining traveling forward or backward in time.

Troubleshoot

Share these tips with your class.

- ✓ Make sure students understand that compound verbs must be parallel and share the same tense.
- ✓ Many people confuse the verbs *lie* and *lay*. *Lie* means "to rest." *Lay* means "to put." The verb *lay* always has a direct object: *Lay the kitten on the bed* is correct; *I will lay down on the bed* is not. This is a case when incorrect usage probably will sound better to your students since they're exposed to it so often in daily speech.

- ✓ Adverbs such as *often, also, already, always, usually* may interrupt the auxiliary and main verbs: *Samson has always had a ferocious roar.* Encourage students to place adverbs before the verb phrase in their writing. This will make it easier for them to identify the complete verb.

Model

Read aloud the passage "Coyote: Fact and Myth" as students read it silently. To show them how you would approach the correction that appears in the passage, you might say: *As I skimmed the first paragraph, I noticed that almost all the verbs are in the present tense. Looking at the third sentence again, I saw the verb phrase "are talking," which is the present tense. "Heard," the past tense of the verb "hear," shouldn't be used. The present tense, "hear," is correct.*

Before students begin reading and correcting the passage on their own, remind them to look for time markers and helping verbs that might be separated from main verbs.

Onward to the Past: **Verb Tenses**

Read the following passage.

Remember: If a sentence has a compound verb, both verbs should be the same tense.

I beg and pleaded, but you won't say anything.

You can beg and plead all you like.

Coyote: Fact and Myth

Have you ever heard the call of coyotes in the middle of the night? At first, you think the sound is a baby crying. Then, you heard more and more cries—almost like the babies are talking to each other. You quickly realize you are hearing the sound of wild animals and not humans. Coyotes howl to contact each other; yelps to celebrate or criticize each other; bark to scare animals away; and huffs to call their pups quietly.

Coyotes can adapting quickly to different habitats. They will change their diet, breeding habits, and social interactions to survive. Keen senses of sight, smell, and hearing enable coyotes to stay alive. These tricky mammals often manage to evade, or avoid, danger. In fact, many Native American cultures has stories about the trickster Coyote.

According to Navajo legend, Coyote is responsible for the scattered appearance of the stars in the sky. Long ago, the First Woman will be creating beautiful patterns in the sky by very carefully placing the stars. Then, Coyote appeared. He begged and begged First Woman to let him help. Although she don't trust Coyote, First Woman eventually agreed. Coyote promised to take his time and do the job right. Of course, that didn't last long. Soon, Coyote got tired and flung the basket of stars across the sky.

So, if you ever hear coyotes howling in the night, look up at the starry sky and thought of the Trickster.

Do you notice any problems in the passage? Are the correct verb tenses used?

Do the verb tenses match the time words in the sentences? Do verb tenses change in the same sentence?

Is a main verb missing its helping verb?

Reread the passage. Then, mark any changes you would make. The first change has been made for you.

Onward to the Past: **Verb Tenses**

Read the checklist at the bottom of the page. Then, go over your revision of "Coyote: Fact and Myth" once more. Copy it on the lines below.

_____

_____

_____

_____

_____

_____

_____

_____

_____

_____

_____

_____

_____

_____

_____

_____

_____

_____

_____

_____

_____

Checklist ....

❑ Have you used the correct verb tense in each sentence?

❑ Does the verb tense shift or change in a sentence?

❑ Are any helping verbs missing in the sentences?

❑ Do the subjects and verbs agree?

Extraordinarily Helpful: ADJECTIVES AND ADVERBS

Adjectives and adverbs bring focus to nouns and verbs by adding details.

Think of the richness that adjectives and adverbs add to our writing. Adjectives expand nouns. Adverbs add verve to verbs, adjectives, and other adverbs.

Your students may encounter the following problems with adjectives and adverbs in their writing:

- Using adjectives instead of adverbs.
- Substituting adverbs for adjectives.
- Choosing the wrong forms of comparative and superlative adjectives and adverbs.

Replay

Use the charts below to review adjectives and adverbs with your class.

	ADJECTIVES	ADVERBS
What They Modify	Nouns	Verbs, Adjectives, Adverbs
Questions They Answer	What kind? *Active* kittens romp. How many? Several kittens snooze. Which ones? *Those* kittens romp.	How? The dogs romped *clumsily*. Where? The kittens romped *outside*. When or How Often? The kittens romped *yesterday*. The kittens romped *frequently*.

POSITIVE ADJECTIVES	COMPARATIVE ADJECTIVES (compare two persons or things)	SUPERLATIVE ADJECTIVES (compare more than two persons or things)
unhappy	unhappier	unhappiest
content	more content	most content
good	better	best

POSITIVE ADVERBS	COMPARATIVE ADVERBS (compare two actions)	SUPERLATIVE ADVERBS (compare more than two actions)
lazily	more lazily	most lazily
well	better	best

Then, have each student write down a noun and a verb on different index cards or pieces of paper. To stretch students' vocabularies, challenge them to come up with really precise and descriptive words. Gather their nouns and verbs. After you read aloud a word, ask students to identify what part of speech it is. Next, give them about 30 seconds to write as many adjectives or adverbs as they can to go with the word. Discuss students' responses in terms of which questions the adjective answers about the noun or which questions the adverbs answer about the verb.

Troubleshoot

Share these tips with your class.

✓ Students may need to be reminded that *scarcely* and *hardly* are double negatives. Point out that in the English language only one negative is used in a sentence. (*That gorilla can hardly stand still* not *That gorilla can't hardly stand still. Scarcely any bananas are hanging from the tree,* not *Scarcely no bananas are hanging from the tree.*)

✓ The correct usage of *good* and *well* often confuses students. *Good* is an adjective, while *well* is an adverb. Point out, however, that *good* appears with sense verbs and *to be* verbs. (*That top spins well. The colors on the top look good when they blend together.*)

Model

Explain to students that they will be reading and revising realistic fiction that has a math theme. Ask them to listen as you read it aloud. Then, discuss the story. As you read, did they catch any adjectives or adverbs that were used incorrectly?

Distribute the passage to students. Go over the correction on the page with them. You might model your response this way: *The correction on the page shows that the word "couldn't" should be "could." I know that neither of these words are adjectives or adverbs, so why was this correction made? What else do I know about the word "couldn't"? It's a contraction for "could not" and "could not" is a negative. I see another negative in the sentence, the word "hardly," which is an adverb. A sentence can't have a double negative in it, so that's why "couldn't" was changed to "could." Another way to revise the sentence would be like this: "Milla couldn't wait to lay out home plate." In that case, the adverb "hardly" was deleted. However, I think that "could hardly wait" shows Milla's eagerness more clearly than "couldn't wait" does.*

Before students complete the revisions independently, you may want to brainstorm a comprehensive list of synonyms for *big* with them, including *large, huge, mammoth, giant, gigantic,* and *enormous.* Remind them of the importance of word variety.

Extraordinarily Helpful: **Adjectives and Adverbs**

Read the following story.

Reminder *Bad* is an adjective. Use *bad* after *to be* verbs *(is, was)*, verbs of sense *(see, feel)*, and verbs of appearance *(look, seem)*.

A Dream Diamond

Once, the vacant lot across the street from Milla's house had been filled with weeds. Now, the level ground was free of weeds. The barely visible outline of a baseball field was drawn in the dirt. Milla couldn't hardly wait to lay out home plate. She consulted the diagram she'd gotten off a baseball Web site the day before.

"The home plate area should be a circle that has a diameter of 26 feet," Milla announced in a loud voice so her more younger brother Sam would hear her. Sam was staggering backward, pretending to catch fly balls.

After home plate, they would create second base. From the back tip of home plate, they'd measure an exactly distance of 127 feet and 3⅜ inches. They were real lucky. Milla's father had plenty of measuring tapes.

"The pitching rubber should be 60 feet and 6 inches from the back tip of home plate," Milla read from the clearly written instructions. "Then, we can measure the distances for first and third bases."

An hour later, they had marked the spot for first base. Milla's mother had carefully stretched a tape measure from second base toward the first base line. Her father had quick stretched a tape measure from the back tip of home plate toward where first base should be.

Milla triumphantly marked the place where the two tape measures intersected at the 90-foot mark. "First base should go right here!"

They repeated the same steps to make third base. "This is beginning to look like a professional baseball field," Sam said in an excitedly voice. "I can't wait to belt a home run out of the park!" He swung an imaginary bat, pretended to fling it to the ground, and then rounded the bases.

Milla waited for her brother at home plate. She pulled a real baseball from behind her back and calmly tagged him. "You're out."

Do you notice any problems in the passage? Are nouns modified by adjectives? Are verbs, adjectives, and adverbs modified by adverbs?

Is the writing as clear as it could be?

Reread the passage. Then, mark any changes you would make. The first change has been made for you.

Revision Mini-Lessons • Grade 5 • Scholastic Teaching Resources

Extraordinarily Helpful: **Adjectives and Adverbs**

Read the checklist at the bottom of the page. Then, go over your revision
of the passage "A Dream Diamond" once more. Copy it on the lines below.

_____

_____

_____

_____

_____

_____

_____

_____

_____

_____

_____

_____

_____

_____

_____

_____

_____

_____

_____

_____

_____

Checklist

❑ Do the adjectives modify nouns?

❑ Do the adverbs modify verbs, adjectives, or adverbs?

❑ Do any of the sentences contain a double negative?

❑ Do adjectives follow *to be* verbs *(is, was)*?

❑ Do adjectives follow sense verbs *(smell, taste, feel, sound, look)* and verbs
of appearance *(look, appear)*?

I See It!: VIVID IMAGES

vivid **adj. 1.** bright and strong: *vivid colors* **2.** forming or giving a clear picture in the mind: *vivid images*

Creating vivid images in writing engages the reader—and the writer. Using active verbs, sensory details, and figurative language gives a writer a unique voice.

Your students may encounter the following problems in incorporating vivid images into their writing:

- Using vague language.
- Repeating the same words.
- Cluttering their work with unnecessary adjectives and adverbs.
- Overloading their work with descriptive elements.

Replay

Select a variety of writing that contains vivid images. As you read a piece aloud, have students shut their eyes and listen. What images did they see as they heard the writer's language? Students may disagree about the images, which is a perfect time to point out that each of us is unique; we all view the world in subtly different ways. It's important for students to realize that each one of them brings this uniqueness to his or her own writing. Then, conduct a brainstorming session in which students revise sentences such as the following to make them more vivid: *It goes fast. They looked good. He saw an animal.*

Troubleshoot

Share these tips with your class.

✓ Creating vivid images begins with choosing strong nouns and verbs. Adding adjectives and adverbs to blah nouns and verbs won't do much to brighten a piece of writing. Visual learners and kinesthetic learners may find it frustrating to create vivid word pictures. Encourage these students by suggesting they first create a visual or tactile representation of an image. Then, discuss their creative processes. To foster a link between the visual or kinesthetic and the verbal, record the descriptive words and phrases they use and talk about this language.

✓ If students are in a language rut, send them to the thesaurus. Keep one handy in your writing center for easy reference. Also remind students that they can access a thesaurus on most computer word processing programs. Emphasize the importance of being selective; rather than drawing attention to itself, a synonym should fit the sentence naturally and enhance the writer's voice.

✓ To give students practice with figurative language, assign a simile or metaphor of the week for them to complete. For example, give them a starter such as *as sweet as . . .* or a model such as *the waves whispered as they hit the beach,* and then have them write their own. Post their work on a Figurative Language bulletin board.

Model

In this passage, students will be replacing existing words with more vibrant or precise ones and adding details to make the writing more vivid. Walk them through the correction on the page: *There's nothing grammatically wrong with this sentence, but it could be written with more verve, more oomph! I like the way that the correction contrasts rich and poor: the richness of the artist's imagination compared to the fact that he doesn't have much money.*

Make sure students understand that the language inside the quotation marks can't be changed since these are John Chamberlain's exact words.

To fire students' imaginations, show them some of John Chamberlain's art. You can find links to images of his work at the ArtCyclopedia Web site **http://www.artcyclopedia.com/artists/chamberlain_john.html**. As an extension, you may want to have students write short descriptive or narrative paragraphs about one of Chamberlain's pieces.

Name _____ Date _____

I See It!: **Vivid Images**

Read the following descriptive essay.

Remember: Always start with strong nouns and verbs. Adding adjectives to a weak noun won't create vivid images. Neither will adding adverbs to a weak verb.

Turning Car Parts Into Art

possess a rich imagination but no money.

Suppose you're a young artist. You∧ ~~don't have very much money.~~ You want to make sculptures by welding big pieces of metal together, but the metal costs too much. What would you do? If you were artist John Chamberlain, you would use any kind of steel you could find. For instance, Chamberlain made sculptures out of metal signs, metal benches, metal sand pails, and metal lunch boxes. The metal had to have color on it. Today, some of John Chamberlain's most famous sculptures are those made from car parts. The steel is colorful and crunched together—bumpers and fenders from different cars welded together.

Auto body shops cut up cars into parts, and Chamberlain would take whatever he wanted from their scrap piles. He describes how he would pick car parts for his art: "I was interested in either the color or the shape or the amount. I didn't want engine parts, I didn't want wheels, upholstery, glass, oil, tires, rubber. . . . Just the sheet metal. It already had a coat of paint on it."

Chamberlain would then cut, crush, and crimp the car parts. He'd spray paint, stencil, and dribble them with paint. One person describes the colors Chamberlain used with these words: *hot, jazzy,* and *tropical.*

So the next time you see an object made out of metal—a sign, a bike, a wagon, a piece of a car—think what kind of sculpture you'd make out of it.

Do you notice any problems in the passage? Can you picture what the writer describes? Can you use these pictures to make the descriptions more vivid? Are the nouns and verbs as strong as they could be?

Do the adjectives and adverbs make the writing more descriptive?

Reread the passage. Then, mark any changes you would make. The first change has been made for you.

I See It!: **Vivid Images**

Read the checklist at the bottom of the page. Then, go over your revision of the passage "Turning Car Parts Into Art" once more. Copy it on the lines below.

_____

_____

_____

_____

_____

_____

_____

_____

_____

_____

_____

_____

_____

_____

_____

_____

_____

_____

_____

Checklist

❏ Have you replaced weak nouns and verbs with stronger ones?

❏ Do the adjectives really serve the nouns? Do the adverbs contribute to the verbs, adjectives, or adverbs?

❏ Have you used too many adjectives and adverbs?

❏ Is the passage clear? Is it interesting to read?

❏ Will the descriptions help readers picture Chamberlain's art?

Strides or Long Steps?: WORD CHOICE

One of the most important elements in clear and vivid writing is word choice. A writer's style is revealed in the words he or she chooses.

Your students may experience the following problems with word choice in their writing:

- Choosing unnecessarily big words instead of shorter and simpler ones.
- Using language that sounds unnatural.
- Repeating words and phrases.
- Inserting unnecessary words.

Replay

There are two important points to keep in mind when you're teaching students about word choice. First, searching for just the right word can be a fun activity. Second, a word should enhance a student's writing voice rather than making it sound forced.

Write two sentences that have the same meaning on the board. Make one sentence brief but energetic and the other sentence convoluted. You might use the following examples:

The toothless, ancient, wrinkled, bald-headed gentleman consumed the piping-hot and sugary sweet, red, cherry turnover.

The man, ancient and bald, quickly gummed the sugary cherry turnover—even though it was hot.

Ask students which sentence they think more clearly describes the man and his actions. Which sentence immediately gave them a vivid mental picture? Then, challenge students to write a sentence that conveys the same meaning as the example sentences. As they share their sentences, point out the similarities and differences in students' word choices. Also, be sure to acknowledge that it is sometimes easy to go overboard when replacing mundane words with more exciting words. In deciding which words to use, writers always strive to make their writing clear and compelling. Inserting a big word does not always add to the clarity of a piece of writing. It's important to applaud the risks that students take in strengthening their writing vocabulary, but it's equally important to help them learn how to refine their word choices.

Troubleshoot

Share these tips with your class.

✓ Errors in speech often appear in students' writing. They record what they hear, for instance, *would of, could of, should of, suppose to,* and *use to.* Spend a few minutes reviewing the proper spelling of these phrases: *would have, could have, should have, supposed to,* and *used to.*

✓ The words *very, really,* and *quite* are often overused. Write several sentences containing these words on the board. Go over them with the class, and then erase the words when they don't add to the clarity of the sentence. Ask students how the deletions affect the sentences and to suggest more exciting replacement words.

✓ Repeating words and phrases can emphasize key points in a piece of writing. However, it's easy to reuse the same words in a sentence or a paragraph unintentionally. Introduce the editorial mark [rep] for repetition to students. Encourage them to mark repeated words and phrases in their writing.

Model

Emphasize that choosing the right word is an important part of every aspect of writing. Peppering writing with large words can make a reader focus on individual words instead of paying attention to the entire work. Before you read aloud the passage, reveal its title and genre. Ask students to predict what they think the story will be about. Talk about the interplay between the words *snagged* and *spiny.* Read aloud the passage as students follow along. Discuss the content and gauge how successful everyone's predictions were. Then, model your response to the correction shown on the page: *Instead of using the word* back *once, it's repeated three times in this first sentence. Let me read it aloud: "Gabe craned his head back, back, back to try to see the top of the prickly pear." I think repeating the word* really *shows how far Gabe had to tilt back his head—and he had to do that because the prickly pear cactus was so unnaturally tall. Most prickly pears don't grow taller than six or seven feet high.*

NOTE: Before reading this passage, you may want to familiarize students with the Chihuahuan Desert and the cactuses mentioned by bringing in images of them. A good resource is the Chihuahuan Desert Research Institute Web site http://www.cdri.org.

Strides or Long Steps?: **Word Choice**

Read the following fantasy.

Reminder: Big words and several adjectives don't always make your writing clear or interesting.

It is really very late. You really should go to sleep. Are you really suffering from a severe case of insomnia?

I *really* can't get any sleep if you don't stop talking.

Caught in the Spiny Forest
back, back

Gabe tilted his head back ^ to try to see the top of the prickly pear. He knew all about cactuses. Hadn't he lived in west Texas in the Chihuahuan Desert all his life? The prickly pear was very tall—but that was impossible. *I'm dreaming,* Gabe thought. *That's what's happening. I'm dreaming.*

Crowded next to the prickly pear's paddles were an ocotillo with tall, thin branches shaped like whips and a plump barrel cactus. The cactuses were so close together that their sharp needles and spines were knit together and blocked Gabe's path. The size of the plants was disturbing, but the number of them was even stranger. Usually in the desert, there was plenty of space between outcroppings of cactus.

Gabe reached out and gingerly manipulated the prickly pear. If the cactuses had gotten so big, what had happened to the spiders and scorpions that lived in the desert? A weapon might come in handy. Gabe grabbed a cactus spine with both hands, swinging on it until he heard a crack. He hit the base of the ocotillo with his new sword. A gigantic moth flew out. Gabe dropped to the ground and covered his head. *This is just a dream. I'll wake up soon.*

Then, the ground began to convulse. A huge wind blew through the spiny forest. The needles of the cactuses clicked against each other. Without looking up, Gabe felt the shadow of a huge bird cover him. The ground heaved, throwing him up and down. *WAKE UP, GAAAAABE!*

Do you notice any problems in the passage? Is the writing clear?

Can you replace any big words with simpler ones? Are any words or phrases repeated too often?

Reread the passage. Then, mark any changes you would make. The first change has been made for you.

Revision Mini-Lessons • Grade 5 • Scholastic Teaching Resources

Strides or Long Steps?: **Word Choice**

Read the checklist at the bottom of the page. Then, go over your revision of "Caught in the Spiny Forest" once more. Copy it on the lines below.

_____

_____

_____

_____

_____

_____

_____

_____

_____

_____

_____

_____

_____

_____

_____

_____

_____

_____

_____

_____

_____

Checklist

❏ Have you used precise language?

❏ Does the writing sound natural?

❏ Can any big words be replaced by shorter words?

❏ Have you repeated any words or phrases?

Revision Mini-Lessons • Grade 5 • Scholastic Teaching Resources

Between You and Me: PREPOSITIONAL PHRASES AND CONJUNCTIONS

Passage "Dolley Madison's White House" (nonfiction: biography) **Curriculum Area** Social Studies

Prepositional phrases can supply more information about nouns, verbs, and adjectives, while conjunctions can connect subjects, verbs, and sentences.

Your students may run into the following problems using prepositional phrases and conjunctions in their writing:

- Using the wrong preposition with a verb.
- Ending a prepositional phrase with a subjective pronoun.
- Joining sentences (independent clauses) without using punctuation or conjunctions.

Replay

Prepositional Phrases: Remind students that a prepositional phrase is a group of words that begins with a preposition. A prepositional phrase can serve as an adjective or an adverb. It always ends with a noun or an objective pronoun (*me, you, him, her, it, us, them*). Problems sometimes crop up when there are two objects of the preposition, and at least one is a pronoun; for example: *My parents bought tickets for Sherri and me.* Many people will rephrase the sentence as *My parents bought tickets for Sherri and I* because they think it sounds more formal, which makes it sound correct. Also, point out that a prepositional phrase does not contain a subject and a verb. Ask students to supply the missing preposition in each sentence below and to identify what each prepositional phrase modifies.

1. I am going _____ the second annual Most Beautiful Goat Contest _____ Cooper's Farm. (*to, adverb phrase modifying "am going"; at, adverb phrase modifying "Contest"*)

2. My cousins Franny and Jason are going _____ the contest _____ me, too. (*to, adverb phrase modifying "are going"; with, adverb phrase modifying "are going"*)

3. The brown-and-white goat _____ the pond has such a shiny coat. (*near, by, or beside; adjective phrase modifying "goat"*)

4. The pure-white goat _____ the barn is the most beautiful goat I've ever seen. (*inside, outside, or in; adjective phrase modifying "[white] goat"*)

Conjunctions: Review the coordinating conjunctions— *and, but, or*—with students. Explain that conjunctions can be used to join subjects, verbs, and sentences. This helps avoid needless repetition and gives writing more variety. Use sentences 1–4 to give students practice in using conjunctions to combine ideas. Ask them to combine and rewrite sentences 1 and 2 and sentences 3 and 4. (*Sample answers: My cousins Franny and Jason and I are going to the Most Beautiful Goat Contest at Cooper's Farm. The brown-and-white goat near the pond has such a shiny coat, but the pure white goat inside the barn is the most beautiful goat I've ever seen.*)

Troubleshoot

Share these tips with your class.

✓ In trying to make their sentences more complex, students often move prepositional phrases far from the words they modify, and it's difficult for the reader to follow the logic of the sentence: *The pure-white goat is the most beautiful goat I've ever seen near the barn.* In this case, the wrong goat is being modified.

✓ When students join sentences, they may forget to add a comma before the coordinating conjunction, omit the coordinating conjunction, or do both. Remedy this by having students identify the subjects and verbs in the sentences. Then, ask them to break the sentence into two separate sentences. Guide students in using a coordinating conjunction, and placing a comma before it, to reconnect the sentences.

Model

After students read "Dolley Madison's White House" to themselves, discuss the content of the biography. Then, call on a volunteer to read it aloud. Ask if anyone had difficulty reading the essay because of the placement of prepositional phrases. Did any of the sentences sound confusing or repetitive?

Think out loud about the correction shown on the page. You might say something like the following: *Sometimes a writer will repeat certain words or phrases for emphasis—to really bring home a point or a feeling. I don't think the repetition in the second sentence does that. It makes the writing seem dull and repetitive. Combining the sentences by combining the adjectives makes sense: "August 23, 1814, was a hot and muggy day in Washington, D.C." I might also have rewritten the sentences like this: "August 23, 1814, was a hot day in Washington, D.C., and it was too muggy." Instead of combining the adjectives, I combined the sentences to emphasize how uncomfortable the day was.*

Between You and Me: PREPOSITIONAL PHRASES AND CONJUNCTIONS

Read the following biography.

Reminder: Conjunctions—*and, or, but*— can be used to connect two sentences, but don't forget to place a comma before the conjunction.

Dolley Madison's White House

and muggy

August 23, 1814, was a hot ∧ day in Washington, D.C. ~~It was muggy in Washington, D.C.~~ From the second floor of the White House, First Lady Dolley Madison turned a spyglass to the east. She turned the spyglass to the north. In all directions she turned the spyglass, looking for the invading British army. A trunk lay open near Dolley's feet. Carefully packed inside it were important government papers. Some of the White House's new treasures—objects made of silver and china—were clustered in a pile. Dolley was going to load them into a wagon. She was going to send the wagon to the Bank of Maryland until the British were forced out of the United States.

The thought of having to flee angered and saddened Dolley. The White House had just been remodeled. Congress had given her a small budget for the job. She had managed to buy simple but beautiful things. The new furnishings truly reflected America's style and ideals.

Suddenly, Dolley spotted black smoke rising of the sky. *There's no time to lose,* she thought. The distance between the British army and she was closing fast. She had one more treasure to save: George Washington's portrait.

Dolley grasped the frame. She tried to pull the portrait from the wall. It wouldn't budge! Dolley gave the order to cut the canvas from its frame. She carried the canvas out of the White House.

The British burned the White House. Thanks to the brave actions in Dolley Madison, many of its treasures were saved.

Do you notice any problems in the passage? Are the correct prepositions and nouns used in the phrases?

Is it clear who or what the phrases modify? Can you combine any subjects, verbs, or sentences? Is the writing as clear as it could be?

Reread the passage. Then, mark any changes you would make. The first change has been made for you.

Between You and Me: **Prepositional Phrases**

Read the checklist at the bottom of the page. Then, go over your revision of "Dolley Madison's White House" once more. Copy it on the lines below.

_____

_____

_____

_____

_____

_____

_____

_____

_____

_____

_____

_____

_____

_____

_____

_____

_____

_____

_____

_____

Checklist

❑ Do prepositional phrases begin with the correct preposition? Do they end with nouns or objective pronouns?

❑ Is it clear which word each phrase is modifying?

❑ Have you combined subjects, verbs, and sentences whenever you could? Have you used the correct conjunction?

❑ Have you placed a comma before a conjunction that joins two sentences?

Short and Long: SENTENCE VARIETY

Passage "A Thief in the Night"
(nonfiction: narrative essay)

Curriculum Area Science

Repeating the same sentence patterns is boring. Varying the length of sentences is more exciting. (Let me revise that.) Repeating the same sentence patterns can bore your readers. If you vary the length and structure of your sentences, you will keep your readers engaged.

Your students may encounter the following problems when it comes to sentence variety:

- Repeating the same sentence pattern.
- Using short, choppy sentences.
- Running sentences together.
- Creating overly complex sentences.

Replay

Write the following sentences on the board, and read them aloud:

Into the air, the lizard jumped. Onto the branch, it leaped. Into the air, the lizard dived. Onto a branch, it jumped. Into the air, the lizard leaped.

Ask students to critique the writing. Encourage them to identify the repeated sentence pattern (prepositional phrase, subject, verb).

Then, ask small groups to work together and revise the sentences to create more variety and interest. Remind them that varying sentence structure, using conjunctions to combine sentences, and adding words will create more interesting prose. To monitor their progress, circulate among the groups. Allow time for all the groups to share their sentences. Comment on any diversities in the revisions, and also point out any similarities.

Troubleshoot

Share these tips with your class. NOTE: Also see the previous mini-lesson on prepositional phrases and conjunctions (page 24) for more troubleshooting tips.

✓ Make sure that students don't abandon short sentences altogether. Sometimes, a writer wants to stop the flow of words and jolt the reader. Remind students that a short sentence can be a good way to grab a reader's attention—as long as short sentences are used sparingly and for good effect. Sentence variety is as important as word choice.

✓ Every piece of writing has its own rhythm. Encourage students to read aloud their writing as they work. With practice, they'll be able to really hear the rhythm of their writing. A sing-song voice can mean that the sentences are too similar. Stumbling in the middle of a sentence or having to go back to the beginning of one can indicate the sentence is too long and convoluted. As you model your own writing for students, be sure to show how you read aloud to find its rhythm.

Model

After students read the passage "A Thief in the Night" to themselves, reread it aloud to them. Briefly discuss the content to make sure everyone understands what's happening in the essay before they begin their revisions. Then, think about the correction shown on the page. For example, you might say the following: *The revision on the page combines two sentences: "I solved it. I used observation." The revision joins the sentences with the preposition "by" and changes the form of the verb from "used" to "using": "I solved it by using observation." I thought about other ways to combine the first three sentences. Here's what I came up with:*

We had a mystery at our house, but I solved it. I used observation.

We had a mystery at our house, but I solved it, and I used observation.

We had a mystery at our house, but I solved it by using observation.

I still like the revision on the page better because the first sentence is dramatic: "We had a mystery at our house." It really pulled me in. Then, the next two sentences tell me that the mystery was solved and how it was solved. I kept reading, however, because I wanted to know what the mystery was and exactly how the writer used observation to solve it.

The point here is to get students to realize that there are many ways sentences can be combined but that each combination may have subtle differences in meaning.

Short and Long: **Sentence Variety**

Read the following narrative essay.

Reminder: Use the conjunctions *and, but,* and or to join sentences and create variety in your writing.

My name is Polly. My feathers are green. My beak is yellow. My—

I know my name, and I'm aware of the colors of my feathers and beak.

A Thief in the Night

We had a mystery at our house. I solved it∧ ⊬used observation. We also had a lot of mosquitoes at our house. That's what caused the mystery. You see, my parents had brought home some mosquito doughnuts. You put half of a doughnut into a small container of water. The doughnuts have a bacteria in them called *bacillus thuringiensis.* Mosquitoes lay their eggs in the water. The bacteria eat up the eggs before they hatch.

Okay, that's enough science. Here's the mystery. Something or someone was turning over the containers. They were spilling the water and the mosquito doughnuts. This happened at night. Every morning, I had to go outside. I had to scoop the doughnuts back into their containers. I had to fill the containers with more water. It got boring. I decided to find out who or what was messing with the containers.

Before I went to bed, I put a container of water near my room. I could see it from my window. The container had a mosquito doughnut in it. Then, I waited. There's a motion-sensor light above my window. If something moves, the light goes on.

Nine o'clock: Nothing happened. Ten o'clock: Nothing happened. Eleven o'clock: Nothing happened. Except I fell asleep. Midnight: Something happened! The outside light went on. There was a loud crash outside my window. I woke up in time to see the black mask of a bandit staring through my window! "It's a raccoon!" I shouted.

The good news is that mosquito doughnuts don't hurt animals, the bad news is that raccoons can get to almost anything. I still have to refill the containers. Every morning, I pour more water into the containers. At least now I know who's to blame.

Do you notice any problems in the passage? Do too many sentences have the same pattern? Are some of the sentences related so you can combine them?

Reread the passage. Then, mark any changes or corrections you would make. The first change has been made for you.

Revision Mini-Lessons • Grade 5 • Scholastic Teaching Resources

Short and Long: **Sentence Variety**

Read the checklist at the bottom of the page. Then, go over your revision of "A Thief in the Night" once more. Copy it on the lines below.

_____

_____
_____
_____
_____
_____
_____
_____
_____
_____
_____
_____
_____
_____
_____
_____
_____
_____
_____
_____

Checklist

❑ Have you used a variety of sentences?

❑ Are too many sentences short and choppy?

❑ Are any sentences too long and confusing?

❑ If you've combined sentences, have you used a conjunction and the proper punctuation?

Revision Mini-Lessons • Grade 5 • Scholastic Teaching Resources

What's the Big Idea?: MAIN IDEA AND DETAILS

Passage "What's in a Name?"
(nonfiction: expository essay)

Curriculum Area Language Arts

A paragraph without a main idea is like a car without a steering wheel. The paragraph, like the car, is likely to move in any direction.

Your students may encounter the following problems with main ideas and details in their writing:

- Omitting a main idea.
- Failing to state a main idea clearly.
- Including unrelated details.
- Failing to use enough details to support the main idea.

Replay

Review the definitions of main idea and details. The main idea is exactly what it sounds like: It's the main, or big, idea of a paragraph or an essay. Details support the main idea. Remind students that a main idea appears at the beginning or near the beginning of a paragraph or an essay. Then, suggest the following main idea and details and challenge students to write a quick paragraph based on them. (Notice that two of the details are irrelevant.) As students reread their work, have them look for unnecessary details. Also, encourage them to add a few more relevant details.

> **Main Idea:** All fifth graders should take bowling lessons.
> **Detail:** Bowling is a healthy activity, so it will make fifth graders fitter.
> **Detail:** There are over 3,000,000 bowlers in the United States.
> **Detail:** Bowlers don't have to worry about the weather when they play.
> **Detail:** Being on a bowling team helps kids learn how to work together.

Troubleshoot

Share these tips with your class.

✓ The key to avoiding major revisions to paragraphs and essays is organization. The more students organize their thoughts before writing, the clearer and more coherent their work will be. As a prelude, consider having students free write their thoughts and questions about a topic. Use outlines and other graphic organizers to help students collect their thoughts before they begin writing.

✓ It can be easy for students to wander from the main idea as they write. For instance, they may treat a supporting detail as a main idea and include other details to support it instead of the true main idea. *The sport of skateboarding was invented in the 1950s. Surfers in California decided to try to surf on the streets. People in Hawaii have been surfing for over 300 years. The first skateboards were boards with roller skates attached to their bottoms.* Each supporting detail must show a strong connection to the main idea. Have students pull out the main ideas and details in their work and plug them into an outline or web to make sure that each detail truly supports the main idea.

Model

Read aloud "What's in a Name?" and then discuss it with students. After students read the passage to themselves, ask them to underline the main idea. In this case, it's the first sentence: "Alan 'Ollie' Gelfand is famous for inventing the ollie."

Then, think aloud to show why the third sentence does not support the main idea. Here's a sample: *After reading the passage, I realized that it wasn't really a biography of Alan "Ollie" Gelfand, but it's really an informative essay describing how he invented a special skateboarding move that is now recognized in the Oxford English Dictionary. What Gelfand does now to earn a living isn't connected to the main idea. Even if it were, the sentence is placed in the wrong place. It interrupts the description of an ollie.* Before students finish editing and revising the passage, remind them to look out for other unnecessary details. You also may want to point out that placing a sentence or phrase within parentheses doesn't mean that the information is irrelevant.

You may want to ask students to find a definition for *ollie* in a dictionary or encyclopedia.

What's the Big Idea?: **Main Idea and Details**

Read the following expository essay.

Reminder: Details should be related, but each one must support the main idea.

A healthy parrot is a happy parrot. Watch out for fluffed up feathers. Make sure your parrot is alert. I feel a little sleepy myself.

Are we talking about you or me?

What's in a Name?

Alan "Ollie" Gelfand is famous for inventing the ollie. In 1976, when Gelfand was a teenager, he figured out a new move on his skateboard. ~~He repairs Volkswagens now.~~ He slammed his back foot down on the tail of the skateboard. That move popped him and his board into the air. Doing an ollie meant that a rider could jump curbs and other objects in the way like fire hydrants and garbage cans. Just by kicking the skateboard against the ground, a rider could literally fly through the air. Soon, skateboarders were using the ollie to do all sorts of tricky moves. Surfers in California invented the skateboard in the 1950s.

Today, Gelfand still does ollies in a 5,000-square-foot warehouse. Inside the warehouse, he's built a large bowl with sloping sides that's perfect for skateboarding. (As a kid in Florida, he and his buddies used to sneak into empty swimming pools. They'd ride their skateboards up and down the sloping sides.) Other famous skateboarders are Tony Hawk and Stacy Peralta.

Thanks to Sharon Israel, who is married to Gelfand, *ollie* has made it into the Oxford English Dictionary (OED). She began to e-mail dictionaries and encyclopedias, asking them to include a definition for *ollie*. Some of the dictionary and encyclopedia editors thought nobody except skateboarders used the word. Then, the Oxford English Dictionary decided to do some research. Its editors searched publications from all over the world, looking for the use of the word. They found *ollie* being used in a variety of ways. In 2004, *ollie* made it into the OED as a noun and a verb.

As Gelfand says, "Once you're in the OED, they can't take you out." In 1976, "Ollie" Gelfand probably had no idea that he'd created a move that would not only affect skateboarding but also our language.

Do you notice any problems in the passage? Is the main idea well stated and easy to identify?

Is the main idea supported by important details?

Reread the passage. Then, mark any changes you would make. The first change has been made for you.

What's the Big Idea?: **Main Idea and Details**

Read the checklist at the bottom of the page. Then, go over your revision of "What's in a Name?" once more. Copy it on the lines below.

_____

_____

_____

_____

_____

_____

_____

_____

_____

_____

_____

_____

_____

_____

_____

_____

_____

_____

_____

_____

_____

_____

Checklist ·

❏ Is the main idea clear and easy to identify?

❏ Do all the details support the main idea?

❏ Are any details unnecessary?

Revision Mini-Lessons • Grade 5 • Scholastic Teaching Resources

Next!: ORGANIZATION

Writing must be clear, concise, and cohesive—no matter what genre the writer chooses.

Your students may encounter the following problems with organization in their writing:

- Placing steps or events out of sequence.
- Failing to use transitional words and phrases or using too many transitions.
- Keeping focus on the topic or theme. (See also the mini-lesson on Main Idea and Details, p. 30.)

Replay

On the day before the mini-lesson, ask students to help you summarize a story they're all familiar with. It may be a classic fairy tale or a story that they have read several times in your class. Record students' contributions on the board. Then, discuss the summary, confirming that the events are in the correct order. Before class begins the next day, copy the summary on a sheet of chart paper, cut apart the sentences, and place them in a paper bag. Call on students to draw sentences. Tape the sentences onto the chalkboard in the order in which they are drawn. Ask student to put the sentences in the proper order. Talk about the strategies they used to piece together the story.

Use any transitional words and phrases in the summary to segue into a review of transitions. You might want to create a reference sheet for students that includes some of the more common transitions; include those that indicate similarity, contrast, sequence and order, time, place and position, cause and effect, emphasis, additional support, and conclusion and summary.

Troubleshoot

Share these tips with your class.

✓ To help students plan their writing, have copies of graphic organizers available. Use main idea and details organizers, webs, and outlines for their nonfiction writing. Provide sequence or story problem-and-solution graphic organizers for their fiction writing. When students have trouble with clarity and cohesion in a piece of writing, encourage them to complete the appropriate graphic organizer for their work.

✓ Let's face it, students resist reading over their work. Completing a first draft can seem like an enormous project to them. It's important, however, to impress upon students the importance of reading their work. Not going over their work is like walking out the door without looking in the mirror. You might also help students designate a trusted reader who can alert them to any organizational problems—and can cheer their writing successes.

Model

Read aloud "Yesterday, I Was an Alien" while students follow along. Discuss the content of the story, emphasizing that even though the passage is fiction, the events still have to be believable and flow in a logical order. Guide students in summarizing the story, and write the summary on the board. Next, model the first correction as follows: *As I read the first paragraph, I realized that the title came from a sentence in the passage. Changing the first sentence to "Yesterday, I was an alien," makes sense. First, it refers back to the title, and second, it makes the first paragraph clear and logical. Just to make sure, I reread the revised first paragraph to myself:* Yesterday, I was an alien. Being an alien always made me feel weird, like people thought I was from Jupiter and had landed in the United States in a space ship or something. Actually, my family moved to Tennessee from Argentina three years ago. *In the revision, the writer states that he or she was an alien, how it felt, and why he or she was an alien. That seems like a more logical order to me.*

Before students finish revising the passage, you may want to point out that sometimes the order of paragraphs may need to be shifted so the organization of the entire story is better. Remind them to look for tell-tale transitions. In this story, the final paragraph should be moved up to become the third paragraph.

Next!: **Organization**

Read the following passage.

Reminder: Be sure to place events in the proper order so your writing will be clear.

Whistle a song. Oh, but before you do that, say "Hello!" No, wait, you should say my name first.

I have no idea what you want me to do.

Yesterday, I Was an Alien

∧ Being an alien always made me feel weird, like people thought I was from Jupiter and had landed in the United States in a space ship or something. Actually, my family moved to Tennessee from Argentina three years ago. Yesterday, I was an alien.

I wasn't thrilled when my parents told me we were all going to become American citizens. Tennessee didn't feel like home to me then—I didn't think Tennessee would *ever* feel like home to me. I can't even begin to tell you how different Tennessee is from Argentina. For one thing, there's the difference in barbecue.

A few months later, we took a citizenship test. My homeroom teacher helped me prepare for it. He taught me a lot about the Constitution and American history. He even gave me extra credit for writing about how it felt to become an American citizen.

This morning, we went down to the courthouse. A judge asked us why we wanted to become U.S. citizens. I told the truth: I like the barbecue in Tennessee better than in Argentina. Now, we're going to celebrate at Smokey Jane's Real Pit BBQ. Everybody laughed, but my answer convinced the judge. She swore us in as American citizens, and we all recited the Pledge of Allegiance.

To start the whole process, we had to fill out a form that asked all kinds of questions. The United States wants to make sure somebody's going to be a good citizen and not cause any trouble. Then, we had to have our fingerprints taken. That was pretty cool. My sister said being fingerprinted made her feel like a criminal instead of an alien.

Do you notice any problems in this passage? Is the writing clear and logical? Are the events in order?

Does the passage need more transitional words or phrases?

Reread the passage. Then, mark any errors you spot or corrections you would make. The first change has been made for you.

Revision Mini-Lessons • Grade 5 • Scholastic Teaching Resources

Next!: **Organization**

Read the checklist at the bottom of the page. Then, go over your revision of "Yesterday, I Was an Alien" once more. Copy it on the lines below.

_____

_____

_____

_____

_____

_____

_____

_____

_____

_____

_____

_____

_____

_____

_____

_____

_____

_____

_____

_____

Checklist ·

❑ Are the events of the story clear?

❑ Do the events unfold in a logical order?

❑ Have you added transitional words and phrases?

35

Who Is It?: VOICE

Everyone's writing voice is unique. We can identify a person by hearing his or her voice, but we also can recognize someone by reading what he or she has written.

Your students may encounter the following problems with voice in their writing:

- Failing to state exactly what they mean.
- Being too wordy.
- Using an inappropriate voice for the type of writing.

Replay

Write several sentences that contain the problems mentioned above on the board or an overhead transparency. Briefly discuss each sentence to make sure students understand the gist of it. Also, guide them to understand the problem with each sentence. Here are some sample sentences you might use.

1. *If they found a broken window, most people would probably come home and think what had happened.* (failing to state exactly what they mean)

2. *Inside the huge and vast hardware store that sells tools and items for the home, workers who have spent many years learning about home repairs spend countless hours telling customers how to fix things, including how to replace and install a window that somebody accidentally broke during a baseball game.* (wordiness)

3. *Repairing stuff is boring.* (inappropriate voice)

For homework, have students paraphrase the sentences. (You might want to model how you would paraphrase a sentence.) Remind students if necessary that paraphrasing is restating a sentence in one's own words. Also, explain that reading one's work aloud can be an important element in strengthening one's writing voice. As students paraphrase the sentences, they should also read aloud what they've written. Does the language sound natural to their ears? Do they trip over any words or phrases? Set aside time the next day for students to share their paraphrases. Be alert for subtle differences in language and phrasing that differentiate students' voices, and point out these differences in their sentences.

Troubleshoot

Share these tips with your class.

✓ Clichés can slip into anyone's writing because they are words and phrases we don't have to give any thought to using. Young students especially can be prone to using clichés because they think the phrases give their writing more weight. Give an example of a cliché such as "as blue as the sky," and challenge students to refresh and update the simile.

✓ Encourage students to strengthen their writing voices by avoiding passive verbs in their writing. Display a Passive Verb versus Active Verb bulletin board giving example sentences for each construction; for example, *The baseball was slugged into the window by my sister. My sister slugged the baseball into the window.* Illustrate the sentences with a drawing of the action. Post a new passive sentence every day, and then have pairs of students collaborate on the revised, active sentences and illustrations.

✓ In addition to reading aloud their work, young writers can gain insight into voice by thinking about their favorite authors and what draws them to certain writers' work. If a student cites a writer's use of dialogue, for instance, have him or her create a short play or a short story that is predominately dialogue.

Model

Ask students to read "The Flat A" independently, and then call on a volunteer to read it aloud to the class. Talk about whether students keep diaries and how they would describe the writing and the voice they use. Did the voice in the passage seem accurate and real to them?

Then, model the change on the page for students: *The great thing about keeping a diary is that a person's voice really comes through. We usually use an informal voice when we keep diaries. We write a lot like we speak. This is called "stream of consciousness." You write what you're thinking without editing yourself. The words "become aware of" sound too formal for this writer's voice. The word "notice" is a better choice. It makes the writing flow better. Now, it's your turn. Remember to start at the beginning of the entry and look for words that don't sound like the writer or sentences that don't fit the overall informal tone of the passage. And, as always, look for writing that isn't clear.*

Who Is It?: **Voice**

Read the following story.

Reminder: Remember—your writing voice is just as distinctive as your speaking voice.

The Flat A

Dear Diary: Last night, I told to you that I'd get Michael Stephens ∧ become aware of [to notice] me in band class. Guess what??? Today, he did! Then, why do I feel so blue about it? Forget feeling blue: I feel humiliated, ashamed, and mortified. Did I mention embarrassed?

As you know, Michael sits right in front of me in band. The flute players sit in front of us clarinet players, which some people think is unfair because they'd rather switch. Michael hasn't turned around once to look at me this whole year. And I was the one who volunteered to show him where the band hall was in September when he was the new kid and didn't know where anything was! Okay, so today in practice, we were playing "The Maple Leaf Rag," which is one of my favorite songs. It's also pretty difficult to play. This ragtime tune was written by Scott Joplin in the early 1900s. The song was so popular that Teddy Roosevelt's daughter, Alice, had it played in the White House.

I guess I got carried away during the song. At the termination of it, Michael turned around and said, "That should have been an A flat, not a flat A, Amber." It <u>was</u> pretty funny, though. That last note just kind of squawked out of my clarinet. Oops—Mom says I have a phone call—later!

Guess who just called? Michael! He said he wanted to apologize. He didn't want things to end on a bad note between us. That provoked a guffaw in me. But I told him how rude I thought he'd been to me all year. He said he thought I'd been ignoring him the whole time!

Do you notice any problems with the passage? Does the writer use too many words or words that don't sound natural? Does the voice change within the story?

Is the writing as clear as it could be?

Reread the passage. Then, mark any changes or corrections you would make. The first change has been made for you.

Who Is It?: **Voice**

Read the checklist at the bottom of the page. Then, go over your revision of "The Flat A" once more. Copy it on the lines below.

_____

_____
_____
_____
_____
_____
_____
_____
_____
_____
_____
_____
_____
_____
_____
_____
_____
_____
_____
_____
_____
_____

Checklist ·

❏ Do some sentences contain too many words?

❏ Does some language sound forced?

❏ Does the voice change within the story?

Make 'em Laugh: PURPOSE AND AUDIENCE

Passage "A Clean Sweep"
(nonfiction: expository essay)

Curriculum Area Science

Students would be disappointed if they went to a soccer game and saw a science fair set up on the field instead. They probably wouldn't stay because they'd been expecting a different experience. This is true with writing, too. Writers need to consider their purpose and audience.

Your students may encounter the following problems with purpose and audience in their writing:

- Straying from their original purpose.
- Using an inappropriate tone to convey their purpose.
- Incorrectly gauging the knowledge of their audience.

Replay

Display a variety of print sources for students to examine—for instance, picture books, chapter books, young adult and adult novels, newspapers, and articles from different special-interest magazines. Ask students to choose one source and then think about why the author wrote it and who its audience might be. As they share their thoughts, have students reveal the clues they used to determine purpose and audience.

Briefly review the different purposes a writer may have—to inform, entertain, and persuade. Remind students that a writer can have more than one purpose but that the purposes have to mesh comfortably within the writing. Including a joke in an expository essay on the Pony Express may or may not work. If the joke is used to make a point about the topic, the audience probably would accept it. However, if the joke is included only as entertainment, a reader would be confused and might even begin to distrust the writer.

Troubleshoot

Share these tips with your class.

✓ Students often tend to lose their voices in expository writing. They feel that reports and informative essays require an excessive formality. Emphasize that their writing voice should remain distinctive and natural. Using big words simply to impress readers will backfire.

✓ The foundation of all good writing is the author's passion about his or her subject. Whenever possible, try to match writing assignments to students' personal interests. If a subject or topic seems dull and boring to students, work with them to find a personal connection to the material that can fuel their enthusiasm. It might be necessary to rethink the topic.

✓ Every writer can benefit from having a trusted reader as an audience. This reader, familiar with the writer's voice, can detect any language that sounds forced. A trusted reader can also tell a writer whether the intended purpose has been achieved. Have the writer's ideas made the crucial transition from his or her head to the page?

Model

Read aloud "A Clean Sweep." Discuss the essay and the fact that it's an expository essay. Ask students what they think the author's purpose was in writing it. What kind of audience do they think the writer pictured as he or she was writing? Have them cite examples from the essay to support their answers. Then, model how you would approach the correction shown on the page: *This is an expository essay. An expository essay informs people by using facts. Its tone is also formal. The sentence that's deleted is the writer's opinion sneaking in. The sentence doesn't have anything to do with the topic of the essay, which is who invented windshield wipers and why she did. As a reader, that sentence made me stop. I didn't know why the writer had included it. The sentence made me lose track of the thread of the essay.*

Make 'em Laugh: **Purpose and Audience**

Read the following expository essay.

Reminder: A writer's purpose for writing should always be clear.

I want you to learn how to say *buenos dias*, but I don't really know why.

Then why should I be interested in learning how to say it?

A Clean Sweep

Think about what would happen if cars didn't have windshield wipers. Drivers wouldn't be able to see in bad weather. Snow would coat their windshields. Heavy raindrops would make it hard to see on the road. More accidents would happen. ~~That might be good news for car repair places.~~ Thanks to Mary Anderson, drivers don't have to worry about snow, ice, and rain on their windshields. In 1903, she invented the windshield wiper.

Anderson had traveled from her home in Alabama to New York City. Riding the streetcars in the city, she noticed that the drivers had to get out often to clean the snow off the windshields. When it rained, they had to open a window and stick their heads out of it to see. Who wants to get all wet like that, even if you are wearing a hat?

Mary Anderson got to work. She designed a swinging arm with a rubber blade. Streetcar drivers could control it from inside their vehicles. They wouldn't have to stop their streetcars anymore in bad weather. If the weather was fine, then the arm could be removed. Personally, that sounds like a lot of work to me.

When Mary Anderson invented windshield wipers, not many people owned cars. Some people even thought that windshield wipers were a terrible idea. They believed the wipers would take drivers' attention from the road. How funny is that? However, by 1913, windshield wipers were standard equipment on all cars. So the next time you're in a car, and the driver has to turn on the windshield wipers, think about Mary Anderson.

Do you notice any problems in this passage? Can you identify the author's purpose for writing it? Was it written for readers like you?

Is the writing as clear as it could be?

Reread the passage. Then, mark any errors you spot or corrections you would make. The first change has been made for you.

Revision Mini-Lessons • Grade 5 • Scholastic Teaching Resources

Make 'em Laugh: **Purpose and Audience**

Read the checklist at the bottom of the page. Then, go over your revision of "A Clean Sweep" once more. Copy it on the lines below.

_____

_____

_____

_____

_____

_____

_____

_____

_____

_____

_____

_____

_____

_____

_____

_____

_____

_____

_____

_____

_____

Checklist ·

❏ Is the purpose of this essay clear? Does the writer want to inform, entertain, or persuade the reader?

❏ Was he or she successful?

❏ Who is the audience? What type of reader does the writer want to reach?

Their or There?: PUNCTUATION AND SPELLING

Passage   "Jean's Beans" (fiction: fairy tale)

Curriculum Area   Social Studies

A writer may have a strong voice and passionate ideas, but readers may not notice— if misspellings and missing punctuation distract them.

Your students may encounter the following problems with punctuation and spelling in their writing:

- Confusing words that are homophones.
- Forgetting to indent paragraphs.
- Failing to capitalize the first word in a sentence and proper nouns.
- Leaving off end punctuation.
- Inserting too many commas or omitting them.

Replay

Punctuation: Write on the board a series of unpunctuated phrases, and add more words until you and your students have successfully created and punctuated a complete sentence. The chart below illustrates an example. Repeat this exercise several times, using interrogatory, imperative, exclamatory, and declarative sentences. Use simple, compound, and complex sentences.

Unpunctuated	Punctuated
six pencils some string and a shoelace	six pencils, some string, and a shoelace
blairs bag contained	Blair's bag contained
blairs bag contained six pencils some string and a shoelace	Blair's bag contained six pencils, some string, and a shoelace.

Spelling: Review homophones with students. Explain that many English words sound the same (or very similar) but have different meanings and spellings. Create a chart of common homophones, such as *it's/its, they're/their/there, who's/whose, to/too/two,* and *then/than.* Point out the difference in the first three sets of homophones: One of the homophones contains an apostrophe because it's a contraction.

Troubleshoot

Share these tips with your class.

✓ Students often are confused about whether to place a comma before the conjunction in a series, for instance, *Stella won a big-screen TV, an SUV, and a trip to Hawaii on the game show.* Encourage the use of the serial comma, where each item in the series is separated by a comma. This will help avoid confusion in sentences such as *My favorite foods are Mexican vanilla ice cream, chicken soup, bread, and macaroni and cheese.*

✓ Punctuating possessive nouns ending in s can pose problems, too. There are conflicting rules about this. Some authorities recommend adding only an apostrophe to a singular possessive noun that ends in s. Others say to add an apostrophe and an s— unless the word following the singular possessive noun begins with an s: *Mars's atmosphere* but *Mars' summer.* Although students should know that there are different opinions about punctuating possessives, for consistency's sake, choose one method of punctuation for your classroom.

Model

Since the focus of this lesson isn't on language, have students read "Jean's Beans" silently. Then, before discussing the content of the passage, remind them that a writer often relates a fairy tale to make a point and that fairy tales also follow a structure, usually beginning with "Once upon a time" and ending with "They lived happily ever after." This passage is a takeoff on the Jack and the Beanstalk story. (You may want to review the rules for punctuating dialogue.) Think aloud to show students how you would have discovered the first error: *The first error occurs in the title. Sometimes, it's easy to forget to proofread the title of our work. In this case, the writer forgot to capitalize the title, and he or she left out the apostrophe to make "Jeans" possessive. By reading ahead, I knew that the name of the main character was Jean, so I also knew that the beans must belong to her.*

Their or There?: **Punctuation and Spelling**

Read the following story.

Reminder: *Here* and *hear* are homophones. The words sound the same, but they have different spellings and different meanings.

jean's beans

Once upon a time, a girl named Jean lived at the base of a towering beanstalk. The plant was so tall that it disappeared into the clouds. Jean wandered what kind of bean plant it was. Was it a black-eyed pea a string bean or a black bean plant.

Three times a day the beanstalk shook. The clouds around the plant thickened and stirred. Then, the beanstalk was quite again.

One day, Jean decided to climb the beanstalk. it was hard work. Just as Jean was pulling herself up the last leaf, the shaking started. Suddenly, a huge foot landed right beside her head. "Hey!" she yelled. "Watch where your going! There's a girl down here!

"Fee-fi-fo-fum! I smell—" a voice thundered.

"Hey! Watch your language!" Jean shouted. "There's a gril down here!"

A gigantic, green hand plucked her up. Jean found herself face to face with a pea-colored giant. "Fee-fi-fo-fum! I smell—" the giant began.

Jean took a deep breathe of courage. "Please, sir, what kind of beans are these?"

"These are my beans. That's what kind of beans these are," the giant muttered.

Jean realized the giant had know idea what kind of beans he was piking. She stole a quick look into the bottom of his basket "I love having cornbread when I eat black-eyed peas." she said.

The giant looked at Jean with suspicion. "What's cornbread?"

Jean promise to gather everyone in the county to make a huge pan of cornbread for him. They did. The giant loved it.

A few years later, a terribel drought hit the land. Crops died, and people were hungry. Only the giant's beanstalk thrived. Looking down, he saw the people suffering. He slowly lowered pod after pod of black-eyed peas? Thanks to the giant, everyone survived the drought. In fact, they all lived happily ever after.

Do you notice any problems in this passage? Are the sentences punctuated correctly? Are there any misspelled words?

Reread the passage. Then, mark any errors you spot or any corrections you would make. The first change has been made for you.

Revision Mini-Lessons • Grade 5 • Scholastic Teaching Resources

Their or There?: **Punctuation and Spelling**

Read the checklist at the bottom of the page. Then, go over your revision of "Jean's Beans" once more. Copy it on the lines below.

_____

_____

_____

_____

_____

_____

_____

_____

_____

_____

_____

_____

_____

_____

_____

_____

_____

_____

_____

_____

_____

_____

_____

Checklist ·

❑ Are all the sentences punctuated correctly? Do they begin with a capital letter? Do they end with the correct punctuation?

❑ Have you used the wrong word or homophone?

❑ Are any words misspelled?

Revision Mini-Lessons • Grade 5 • Scholastic Teaching Resources

Answer Key Sample revisions are given.

Subject-Verb Agreement, p. 7

Christmas Eve in Death Valley

The year is 1849. Gold has been discovered in California. It isn't easy for the Forty-Niners, the people heading west to make their fortunes, to reach California. Deserts and the High Sierra Mountains stand between them and California—and nobody wants to get trapped in the Sierras by heavy snowfall.

The members of one wagon party decide to take a chance. Instead of waiting all winter in Salt Lake City and then crossing the mountains, they decide to take the Old Spanish Trail around the mountains. Unfortunately, no wagon train has ever tried this route—and only one person in Salt Lake City knows the trail. Still, the 120 wagons head out, moving slowly—too slowly for some people. When a man rides into camp and shows them a map with a shortcut, almost everyone decides to take another chance. The shortcut would take 500 miles off their trip. Who wouldn't agree to that?

Soon, the group faces Beaver Dam Wash near the present-day border of Utah and Nevada. The sight of this canyon is enough to send 100 wagons back to the Old Spanish Trail. After the remaining 20 wagons make it through the canyon, trouble strikes again. The man—and his map—disappear from camp! Still, the group decides to keep heading west across the desert.

On Christmas Eve, the Forty-Niners camp near springs that spout more than 2,000 gallons of water a minute. They've been traveling across the desert for more than two months. As they leave the springs, one man looks back and says, "Good-bye, Death Valley!" What he doesn't know is that the worst part of the trip still lies ahead. Standing in their path is a wall of mountains.

Noun-Pronoun Agreement, p. 10

Can I Have Another Slice?

A white cloud puffed out of the cement mixer as Mr. Baines emptied the last 50-pound sack of flour into the cement mixer. Soon, pizza dough chugged out of the machine. "I told you math could be fun," Mr. Baines shouted to me as I helped him push the dough to the edges of the specially made pan.

Bettina opened the last huge can of tomato sauce. "I can't believe how sore my arm is," she said. "Who knew that slicing 20 pounds of mozzarella cheese and five pounds of pepperoni could be such hard work?" (Bettina's parents owned a grocery store, and they had donated the tomato sauce, so it was only right that she should get to open the last can.)

The idea of making a super-size pizza came up in Mr. Baines's math class. (It must be the hungriest class in the entire school.) We students figured that we'd be able to cut our pizza into 225 slices. If we sold each slice for two dollars, we'd be able to raise almost $500 for the school library.

Jacob and Madison used brand-new mops to spread tomato sauce on their side of the dough. Then I threw pepperoni rounds on top of the pizza as if I were throwing my Frisbee. Bettina stood beside me and tossed handfuls of grated cheese on top of the pizza.

The pizza tasted great, and we sold every slice. In fact, I bought and ate six slices. Just don't expect me to be having pizza anytime soon.

Verb Tenses, p. 13

Coyotes: Fact and Myth

Have you ever heard the call of coyotes in the middle of the night? At first, you think the sound is a baby crying. Then, you hear more and more cries—almost like the babies are talking to each other. You quickly realize you are hearing the sound of wild animals, not human beings. Coyotes howl to contact each other; yelp to celebrate or criticize each other; bark to scare animals away; and huff to call their pups quietly.

Coyotes can adapt quickly to different habitats. They will change their diet, breeding habits, and social interactions to survive. Keen senses of sight, smell, and hearing enable coyotes to stay alive. These tricky mammals often manage to evade, or avoid, danger. In fact, many Native American cultures have stories about the trickster Coyote.

According to Navajo legend, Coyote is responsible for the scattered appearance of the stars in the sky. Long ago, the First Woman was creating beautiful patterns in the sky by very carefully placing the stars. Then, Coyote appeared. He begged and begged First Woman to let him help. Although she didn't trust Coyote, First Woman eventually agreed. Coyote promised to take his time and do the job right. Of course, that didn't last long. Soon, Coyote got tired and flung the basket of stars across the sky.

So, if you ever hear coyotes howling in the night, look up at the starry sky and think of the Trickster.

Adjectives and Adverbs, p. 16

A Dream Diamond

Once, the vacant lot across the street from Milla's house had been filled with weeds. Now, the level ground was free of weeds. The barely visible outline of a baseball field was drawn in the dirt. Milla could hardly wait to lay out home plate. She consulted the diagram she'd gotten off a Web site the day before.

"The home plate area should be a circle that has a diameter of 26 feet," Milla announced in a loud voice so her younger brother Sam would hear her. Sam was staggering backward, pretending to catch fly balls.

After home plate, they would create second base. From the back tip of home plate, they'd measure an exact distance of 127 feet and 3⅜ inches. They were really lucky. Milla's father had plenty of measuring tapes.

"The pitching rubber should be 60 feet and 6 inches from the back tip of home plate," Milla read from the clearly written instructions. "Then, we can measure the distances for first and third bases."

An hour later, they had marked the spot for first base. Milla's mother had carefully stretched a tape measure from second base toward the first base line. Her father had quickly stretched a tape measure from the back tip of home plate to where first base should be.

Milla triumphantly marked the place where the two tape measures intersected at the 90-foot mark. "First base should go right here!"

They repeated the same steps to make third base. "This is beginning to look like a professional baseball field," Sam said in an excited voice. "I can't wait to belt a home run out of the park!" He swung an imaginary bat, pretended to fling it to the ground, and then rounded the bases.

Milla waited for her brother at home plate. She pulled a baseball from behind her back and calmly tagged him. "You're out."

Vivid Images, p. 19

Turning Car Parts Into Art

Suppose you're a young artist. You possess a rich imagination but no money. You want to create sparks in the art world by welding big pieces of metal together, but metal costs too much. What would you do? If you were artist John Chamberlain, you would use any kind of steel you could get your hands on. For instance, Chamberlain created sculptures out of metal signs and benches, and discarded sand pails and lunch boxes. The only rule was that the metal had to have color on it. Today, some of John Chamberlain's most famous sculptures are those made from car parts. The steel is colorful and crunched together, bumpers and fenders from different cars—a cream-colored door here, a shiny black rear fender there—welded together.

Auto body shops cut up abandoned cars into parts, and Chamberlain would take whatever he wanted from their scrap piles. He describes how he would choose car parts for his art: "I was interested in either the color or the shape or the amount. I didn't want engine parts, I didn't want wheels, upholstery, glass, oil, tires, rubber. . . . Just the sheet metal. It already had a coat of paint on it."

Chamberlain would then cut, crush, and crimp the car parts. He'd also adorn their surfaces by spray painting, stenciling, and dribbling them with colorful, neon-bright paint. One person describes the colors Chamberlain used with these words: *hot, jazzy,* and *tropical*.

So the next time you see an object made out of metal—a rusted stop sign, an abandoned bike frame, a toy wagon with one spinning wheel, a dented car door—imagine what kind of sculpture you'd produce.

Word Choice, p. 22

Caught in the Spiny Forest

Gabe tilted his head back, back, back to try to see the top of the prickly pear. He knew all about cactuses. Hadn't he lived in west Texas in the Chihuahuan Desert all his life? The prickly pear must be over a hundred feet tall—but that was impossible. *I'm dreaming*, Gabe thought. *That's what's happening. I'm dreaming*.

Crowded next to the prickly pear's rounded paddles were an ocotillo with tall, thin branches shaped like whips and a plump barrel cactus. The cactuses were so close together that their sharp needles and spines were knit together and blocked Gabe's path. The size of the plants was disturbing, but the number of them was even stranger. Usually in the desert, there was plenty of space between outcroppings of cactus.

Gabe reached out and gingerly touched the prickly pear. If the cactuses had gotten so big, what had happened to the tarantulas and scorpions that lived in the desert? A weapon might come in handy. Gabe grabbed a cactus spine with both hands, swinging on it until he heard a sharp crack. He whacked the base of the ocotillo with his makeshift sword. A gigantic moth flew out. Dropping to the ground, Gabe covered his head. *This is just a dream. I'll wake up soon.*

Then, the ground began to vibrate. A hot wind pushed through the spiny forest. The needles of the cactuses clicked against each other. Without looking up, Gabe felt the cool shadow of a huge bird cover him. The ground heaved, throwing him up and down. *WAKE UP, GAAAAABE!*

Answers (Continued)

Prepositional Phrases and Conjunctions, p. 25

Dolley Madison's White House

August 23, 1814, was a hot and muggy day in Washington, D.C. From the second floor of the White House, First Lady Dolley Madison turned a spyglass to the east and the north. She turned the spyglass in all directions, looking for the invading British army. A trunk lay open near Dolley's feet. Carefully packed inside it were important government papers. Some of the White House's new treasures—objects made of silver and china—were clustered in a pile. Dolley was going to load them into a wagon and send it to the Bank of Maryland until the British were forced out of the United States.

The thought of having to flee angered and saddened Dolley. The White House had just been remodeled. Congress had given her a small budget for the job, but she had managed to buy simple but beautiful things. The new furnishings truly reflected America's style and ideals.

Suddenly, Dolley spotted black smoke rising in the sky. *There's no time to lose*, she thought. The distance between the British army and her was closing fast. She had one more treasure to save: George Washington's portrait.

Dolley grasped the frame and tried to pull the portrait from the wall. It wouldn't budge! Dolley gave the order to cut the canvas from its frame. She carried the canvas out of the White House.

The British burned the White House, but thanks to the brave actions of Dolley Madison, many of its treasures were saved.

Sentence Variety, p. 28

A Thief in the Night

We had a mystery at our house. I solved it by using observation. We also had a lot of mosquitoes at our house, and that's what caused the mystery. You see, my parents had brought home some mosquito doughnuts. You put half of a doughnut into a small container of water. The doughnuts have a bacteria in them called *bacillus thuringiensis*. When mosquitoes lay their eggs in the water, the bacteria eat up the eggs before they hatch.

Okay, that's enough science. Here's the mystery. Something or someone was turning over the containers at night and spilling the water and the mosquito doughnuts. Every morning, I had to go outside and scoop the doughnuts back into their containers. Then, I had to fill the containers with more water. It got boring. I decided to find out who or what was messing with the containers.

Before I went to bed, I put a container of water with a mosquito doughnut outside my window. There's a motion-sensor light above my window. If something moves, the light goes on. Then, I waited.

Nine o'clock: Nothing happened. Ten o'clock: Nothing happened. Eleven o'clock: Nothing happened—except I fell asleep. Midnight: Something happened! The outside light went on! There was a loud crash outside my window! I woke up in time to see the black mask of a bandit staring through my window! "It's a raccoon!" I shouted.

The good news is that mosquito doughnuts don't hurt animals. The bad news is that raccoons can get to almost anything. Every morning, I still have to refill the containers with more water. At least now I know who's to blame.

Main Idea and Details, p. 31

What's in a Name?

Alan "Ollie" Gelfand is famous for inventing the ollie. In 1976, when Gelfand was a teenager, he figured out a new move on his skateboard. He slammed his back foot down on the tail of the skateboard. That move popped him and his board into the air. Doing an ollie meant that a rider could jump curbs and other objects that got in the way like fire hydrants and garbage cans.

Just by kicking the skateboard against the ground, a rider could literally fly through the air. Soon, skateboarders were using the ollie to do all sorts of tricky moves.

Today, Gelfand still does ollies in a 5,000-square-foot warehouse. Inside the warehouse, he's built a large bowl with sloping sides that's perfect for skateboarding. (As a kid in Florida, he and his buddies used to sneak into empty swimming pools. They'd ride their skateboards up and down the sloping sides.)

Sometimes, a word like *ollie* remains a slang word. However, thanks to Sharon Israel, who is married to Gelfand, *ollie* has made it into the Oxford English Dictionary (OED). She began to e-mail dictionaries and encyclopedias, asking them to include a definition for *ollie*. Some of the dictionary and encyclopedia editors thought nobody except skateboarders used the word. Then, the Oxford English Dictionary decided to do some research. Its editors searched publications from all over the world, looking for the use of the word. They found *ollie* being used in a variety of ways. In 2004, *ollie* made it into the OED as a noun and a verb.

In 1976, "Ollie" Gelfand probably had no idea that he'd created a move that would not only affect skateboarding but also our language.

Organization, p. 34

Yesterday, I Was an Alien

Yesterday, I was an alien. Being an alien always made me feel weird, like people thought I was from Jupiter and had landed in the United States in a space ship or something. Actually, my family moved to Tennessee from Argentina three years ago.

I wasn't thrilled when my parents told me we were all going to become American citizens. Tennessee didn't feel like home to me then—I didn't think Tennessee would *ever* feel like home to me. I can't even begin to tell you how different Tennessee is from Argentina. For one thing, there's the difference in barbecue.

To start the whole process, we had to fill out a form that asked all kinds of questions. The United States wants to make sure somebody's going to be a good citizen and not cause any trouble. Then, we had to have our fingerprints taken. That was pretty cool, although my sister said being fingerprinted made her feel like a criminal instead of an alien.

A few months later, we took a citizenship test. My homeroom teacher helped me prepare for it. He taught me a lot about the Constitution and American history. He even gave me extra credit for writing about how it felt to become an American citizen.

Finally, this morning, we went down to the courthouse. A judge asked us why we wanted to become U.S. citizens. I told the truth: I like the barbecue in Tennessee better than in Argentina. Everybody laughed, but my answer convinced the judge. She swore us in as American citizens, and we all recited the Pledge of Allegiance. Now, we're going to celebrate at Smokey Jane's Real Pit BBQ.

Voice, p. 37

The Flat A

Dear Diary: Last night, I told you that I'd get Michael Stephens to notice me in band class. Guess what??? Today, he did! Then, why do I feel so blue about it? Forget feeling blue, I feel humiliated, ashamed, and mortified. Did I mention embarrassed?

As you know, Michael sits right in front of me in band. The flute players sit in front of us clarinet players. Michael hasn't turned around once to look at me this whole year. And I was the one who volunteered to show him where the band hall was in September when he was the new kid and didn't know where anything was! Okay, so today in practice, we were playing "The Maple Leaf Rag," which is one of my favorite songs. It's also pretty difficult to play. It's a ragtime tune was written by Scott Joplin in the early 1900s.

I guess I got carried away during the song. At the end of it, Michael turned around and said, "That should have been an A flat, not a flat A, Amber." It was pretty funny, though. That last note just kind of squawked out of my clarinet. Oops—Mom says I have a phone call—later!

Guess who just called? Michael! He said he wanted to apologize. He didn't want things to end on a bad note between us. That made me laugh. But I told him how rude I thought he'd been to me all year. He said he thought I'd been ignoring him the whole time!

Purpose and Audience, p. 40

A Clean Sweep

Think about what would happen if cars didn't have windshield wipers. Drivers wouldn't be able to see in bad weather. Snow would coat their windshields. Heavy raindrops would make it hard to see on the road. More accidents would happen. Thanks to Mary Anderson, drivers don't have to worry about snow and rain on their windshields. In 1903, she invented the windshield wiper.

Anderson had traveled from her home in Alabama to New York City. Riding the streetcars in the city, she noticed that the drivers had to get out often to clean the snow off the windshields. When it rained, they had to open a window and stick their heads out of it to see.

Mary Anderson got to work. She designed a swinging arm with a rubber blade. Streetcar drivers could control it from inside their vehicles. They wouldn't have to stop their streetcars anymore in bad weather. If the weather was fine, then the arm could be removed.

When Mary Anderson invented windshield wipers, not many people owned cars. Some people even thought that windshield wipers were a terrible idea. They believed the wipers would take drivers' attention from the road. However, by 1913, windshield wipers were standard equipment on all cars. So the next time you're in a car, and the driver has to turn on the windshield wipers, think about Mary Anderson.

Punctuation and Spelling, p. 43

Jean's Beans

Once upon a time, a girl named Jean lived at the base of a towering beanstalk. The plant was so tall that it disappeared into the clouds. Jean wondered what kind of bean plant it was. Was it a black-eyed pea, a string bean, or a black bean plant?

Three times a day the beanstalk shook. The clouds around the plant thickened and stirred. Then, the beanstalk was quiet again.

One day, Jean decided to climb the beanstalk. It was hard work. Just as Jean was pulling herself up the last leaf, the shaking started. Suddenly, a huge foot landed right beside her head. "Hey!" she yelled. "Watch where you're going! There's a girl down here!"

"Fee-fi-fo-fum! I smell—" a voice thundered.

"Hey! Watch your language!" Jean shouted. "There's a girl down here!"

A gigantic, green hand plucked her up. Jean found herself face to face with a pea-colored giant. "Fee-fi-fo-fum! I smell—" the giant began.

Jean took a deep breath of courage. "Please, sir, what kind of beans are these?"

"These are my beans. That's what kind of beans these are," the giant muttered.

Jean realized the giant had no idea what kind of beans he was picking. She stole a quick look into the bottom of his basket. "I love having cornbread when I eat black-eyed peas," she said.

The giant looked at Jean with suspicion. "What's cornbread?"

Jean promised to gather everyone in the county to make a huge pan of cornbread for him. They did. The giant loved it.

A few years later, a terrible drought hit the land. Crops died, and people were hungry. Only the giant's beanstalk thrived. Looking down, he saw the people suffering. He slowly lowered pod after pod of black-eyed peas. Thanks to the giant, everyone survived the drought. In fact, they all lived happily ever after.